Hocker

Great Tales from Long Ago
THE STORY OF THE VIKINGS

Written and illustrated by Chris Molan

TORSTAR BOOKS
NEW YORK · TORONTO

Note: The Greenland Vikings discovered Vinland in 985/6, and the great stories of their voyages and settlements in the New World were told in *Grænlendinga Saga* (first written down in the late 12th century) and *Eirik's Saga* (mid-13th century). Our text, illustrations and setting are based on the modern translations of the sagas by Magnus Magnusson and Hermann Pálsson, published in 1965 under the title of *The Vinland Sagas*.

The ships shown in the story are based upon the famous ocean-going Gokstad ship in the Oslo Museum, Norway. House interiors and artifacts are largely based on those exhibited at the Jorvik Viking Centre in York.

ED

GREAT TALES FROM LONG AGO
THE STORY OF THE VIKINGS

Torstar Books Inc, 41 Madison Avenue, Suite 2900, New York, NY 10010 by arrangement with Belitha Press Ltd.
Copyright © in this format Belitha Press Ltd, 1986
Text and illustrations copyright © Chris Molan, 1985
Conceived and designed by Belitha Press Ltd, 2 Beresford Terrace, London N5 2DH.

All rights reserved. No part of this book may be reproduced or utilized in any form or by any means, electronic or mechanical, including photocopying, recording, or by any information storage and retrieval system, without permission in writing from the Publisher.
Library of Congress Cataloging in Publication Data:

ISBN 1-55001-032-8
10 9 8 7 6 5 4 3 2 1
Printed in Belgium

THERE WAS A TIME, LONG AGO, WHEN THE NAME "VIKING" struck terror into the hearts of people in many lands.
The Vikings were a bold, sea-faring people, greatly feared for their cruel, murderous raiding.
Each summer, Viking explorers and warriors set sail from their homes in Norway.
Merchants, farmers, and craftsmen followed, braving the open sea in search of new lands where they could trade and settle their families and livestock.

Erik the Red was one of the first great Viking explorers.
He sailed to Greenland, far away to the west.

Leif, Erik's eldest son, wanted to explore the world also. One day, a sailor called Bjarni was talking, and Leif listened, thoughtfully. "When I was young," said Bjarni, "I was sailing to Greenland when my ship became lost in fog. We drifted about for many days, and at last the fog cleared. Before my eyes was a strange new land, covered in forest."

But Bjarni had not stayed to explore, and for this the people mocked him on his return to Greenland. "Now I will be the man to explore this new land," thought Leif Eriksson, and he decided to buy Bjarni's ship.

Soon after, Leif and his crew of thirty-five men set out from Greenland, heading westward across the Northern Sea.

AFTER MANY DAYS THEY SAW STRANGE MOUNTAINS AHEAD. Sailing closer into the chill shadow of mighty glaciers, Leif saw that it was a rocky and barren wasteland.

As they waded ashore, Leif laughed,
"We have done better than Bjarni," he said,
"At least we have set foot on this land."
And he named the country "Helluland," meaning "slab land."
But Leif remembered Bjarni's words as they sailed
further south, for now they saw a sandy coastline,
flat and wooded. Leif called this place
"Markland" or "forest-land."

It was a warmer wind that swelled the sail of their ship, as they steered ever southward. At last they anchored near an island.

THE GREENLAND VIKINGS WERE STIFF AND WEARY after weeks spent in a cramped ship with nothing but stale water to drink.

As they came ashore they saw dew glistening on the grass. They put it to their lips, and it seemed the sweetest thing they had ever tasted.

Looking around them, Leif's men saw tall forests of timber and rolling grasslands which could support sheep and cattle.

"Bring your bedding ashore," called Leif. "We'll make camp here." Soon they found rivers, full of the biggest salmon they had ever seen.

As they made camp, it seemed, too, that the daylight lasted much longer than it had in Greenland. "We shall tell our people that this will be a fine land for them," said Leif, and he decided to build houses and spend the winter there.

THE SOUND OF CRASHING TREES SOON FILLED THE WOODS as Leif's men set to work. They cut timber to build a great hall and cut turf for the walls of their houses. One evening as they labored, they did not notice that one man, a German, was missing. Suddenly he came running toward them, babbling with excitement.
"I've found vines," he said, "vines and grapes!"
"Can it be true?" asked Leif.
"Of course it's true," he answered indignantly. "There were plenty of vines and grapes in Germany, where I was born."

Each day after that the men worked harder still, cutting grapes as well as timber, so that they would have a splendid cargo to take back to Greenland in the spring.

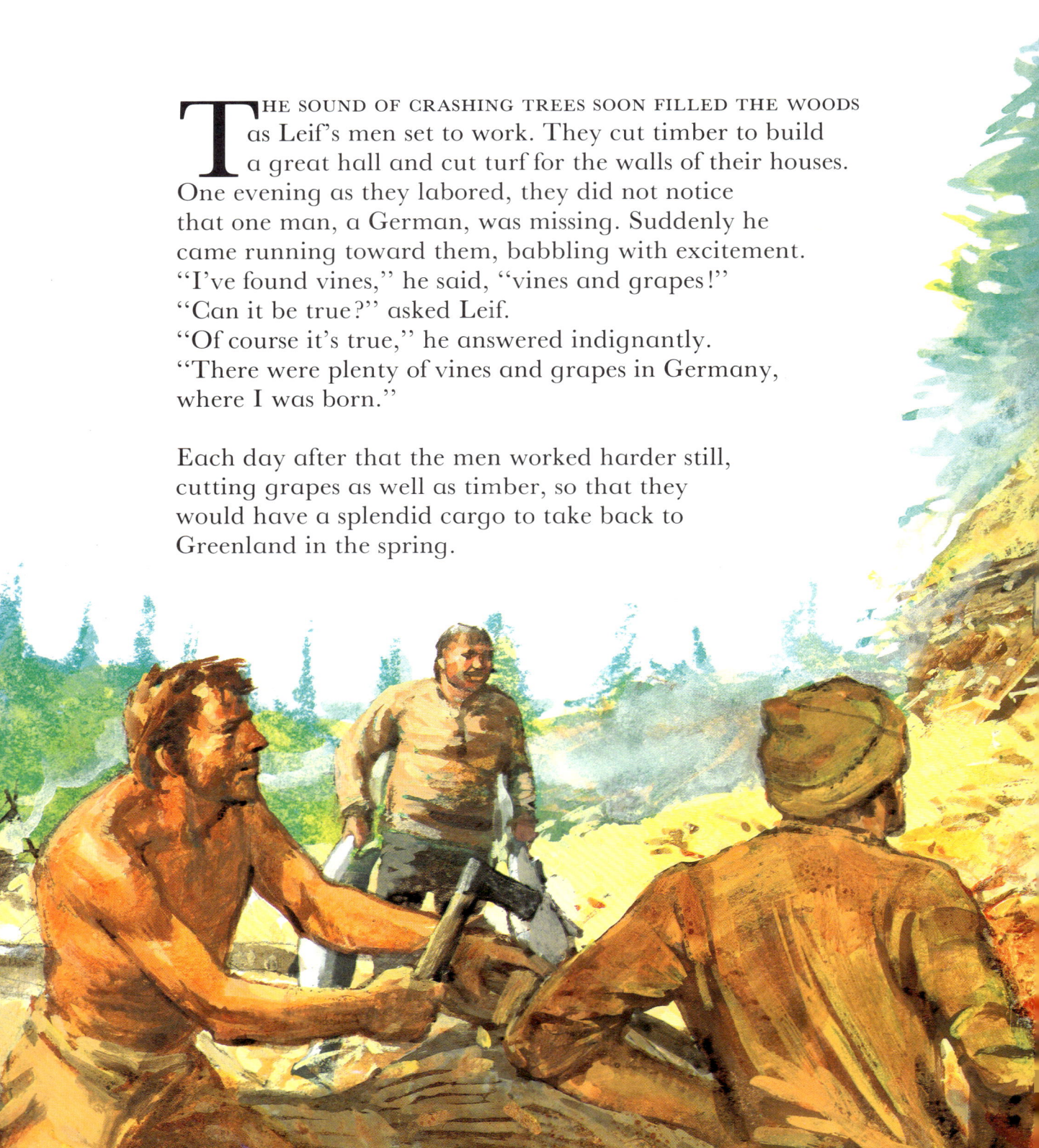

From this time on, Leif named the country "Vinland" – meaning "land of wine-berries."

WITH A RICH CARGO,
the Greenlanders set out on their return journey.
Soon the mountains of their homeland came into view.
But just then, something caught Leif's eye.
On a nearby reef clung the survivors of a shipwreck,
frightened and calling for help.
Swiftly, Leif sent out a boat to bring them all to safety.

Among those rescued was a young woman called Gudrid. From this time forward Leif became known as "Leif the Lucky" – meaning a person of destiny.

LIEF HAD TWO BROTHERS, THORVALD AND THORSTEIN.
When Thorvald heard about Leif's discovery he, too,
went to Vinland, but met with hostile people there,
and was killed by them in battle.
Now Thorstein, in his turn, was eager to follow and
to bring back Thorvald's body to Greenland.
He asked the young woman, Gudrid, to go with him as his wife.
Gudrid was not only young and beautiful,
she was also clever, courageous and determined.
At least she agreed to go with him on his hazardous journey.

ALL THAT SUMMER, THORSTEIN'S SHIP WAS TOSSED BY STORMS. Instead of reaching Vinland they were blown back and forth across the ocean. At last, exhausted, they turned back, to Greenland. As winter approached Gudrid and Thorstein gladly took shelter with a couple at Eriksfjord on the wild Greenland coast.

I CE LAY LIKE A HEAVY COAT OF STEEL OVER GREENLAND THAT WINTER. There was much hunger and disease. Soon it reached the house where Gudrid and Thorstein were staying. Thorstein became ill, and not long afterward, he died. Gudrid was grief-stricken, but on the same night that Thorstein died a strange thing happened.

The household was a pagan one, where the old Viking gods, Thor and Odin, were worshipped. Christianity was still a new religion in Greenland at that time. As Gudrid wept, the wind howled around the house. Just then, the spirit of Thorstein spoke:

> "I have this to say to you Gudrid. You will marry an Icelander and your descendants will be many. Some of them will be great men. One day you will go on a pilgrimage to Rome and return to Iceland where you will become a nun for the rest of your days."

G UDRID WENT TO STAY WITH LEIF'S FAMILY AT THEIR HOME near Eriksfjord, and it was there the following autumn that the prophesy began to come true.
A wealthy merchant from Iceland brought his ship into the harbor.
His name was Thorfinn Karlsefni and
he too was given shelter at Leif's house.
Before long, Karlsefni and Gudrid fell in love,
and they became engaged.

News of the match delighted everyone and it was decided to have the wedding in mid-winter, which was a great time for feasting. The pagan winter festival had now become a Christian one – Christmas. Amid the games and drinking and the telling of tall tales, there was much talk of Vinland.

GUDRID AND KARLSEFNI WERE EAGER TO MAKE A HOME IN "Vinland the Good" as it was now called. So a great expedition was planned, with enough provisions and livestock for the Greenland Vikings to start a new colony. They took all the things they would need – plows and seed, looms for weaving, sleds, tools and weapons.

With a keen wind behind them, Markland soon came into view. After two more days they came to another land, and a stretch of beach so long that they called it "Furdustrands" or "marvel strands."
It was autumn, and being ocean-weary, Karlsefni's expedition set up their camp beside an estuary.

Here Gudrid gave birth to a son, Snorri,
at the beginning of a cruel winter.
The Greenlanders were often hungry
for lack of fresh meat.
This could not be Leif's Vinland.
When spring came Karlsefni decided to seek
for Vinland in the South,
but one man chose to go farther north.
His name was Thorhall,
an ill-tempered warrior.

Now, as he departed, Thorhall said:

*"These oak-hearted warriors
lured me to this land
with promise of choice drinks;
Now I could curse this country!
For I, the helmet-wearer,
must now grovel at a spring
and wield a water-pail;
No wine has touched my lips."*

KARLSEFNI'S EXPEDITION MOVED FARTHER SOUTH AND BUILT their homes beside a tidal lake. Wheat and grapes were plentiful and they called the place "Hope."

One day, a horde of skin-boats suddenly appeared.
They were paddled by small men who waved curious rattling sticks.
Karlsefni went to meet them with a white shield,
as a token of peace.
In that instant a bullock broke loose, bellowing and
causing panic. But quickly the women came forward
and offered milk to the newcomers.

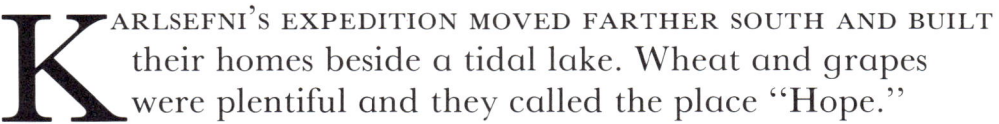

As soon as they tasted it, they were eager to trade,
laying down fine pelts and furs in exchange for
milk and small strips of red cloth.

The cloth began to run short and strips of it were cut even smaller for trade.
The Skraelings – or wretches – as the Greenlanders now called them, knew they were being cheated and became angry.

It was not long before the Skraelings attacked the settlement. Karlsefni's men watched and waited as they swarmed up the estuary, the forest ringing with their terrible war-cries. With crushing, clattering strokes, stone axes and war-clubs fell on wooden shields and Viking swords made of iron.
It was a ferocious battle, but stone was no match for the cruel cut of an iron blade and many Skraelings died. At length a Skraeling leader picked up a fallen Viking axe and examined it. He struck at a tree-trunk to test its strength, then hurled it far out into the lake.
At this the Skraelings fled.

THE PEACE LASTED THROUGHOUT THE WINTER
but there was little cause for festivity that Christmas.
Although the land was so good in every way,
the Greenlanders knew they would
never be able to live there in safety
for they were far outnumbered by the Skraelings.

They got ready to leave Vinland, burying at last
the ashes of their fires. In the springtime when
Gudrid and Karlsefni left Vinland, Snorri was three
years old. He was the first Vinland Viking.

After many more adventures, Karlsefni's expedition returned safely to a great welcome at Eriksfjord in Greenland. Everyone marveled at their cargo of furs and grapes, maplewood and timber, and many fine tales were told that winter at Leif's farmhouse.

This is a map of the journey which Leif and Karlsefni made to Vinland.

As for Gudrid, everything that had been prophesied came true. Gudrid and Karlsefni returned to Iceland and had many fine children. After Karlsefni's death, Gudrid made a journey to Rome and upon her return she became a nun. Snorri built a church in Iceland and two of his grandsons, Bjorn and Brand, became bishops there, as Thorstein had foretold.